Challenger

America's Favorite Eagle

Margot Theis Raven

In cooperation with the American Eagle Foundation

Illustrated by Gijsbert van Frankenhuyzen

* * *

In the late 1700s, there were as many as 300,000 to 500,000 bald eagles in what is now the lower 48 states. By the early 1960s, there were as few as 400 nesting pairs in that territory. Eagles were hunted, killed, and harassed, but the greatest danger to them came from pesticides poisoning the environment.

To Mimi, who told me stories about the birds when I was small, and to my brother, Bob,
who sat with me on our grandmother's "mountain" knees, loving her every word.

Margot

To Dr. James Sikarskie for his efforts to help raptors through his teaching and care at the
Michigan State University College of Veterinary Medicine's Wildlife Rehabilitation Center,
as well as over 30 years of research with the American bald eagle.

Gijsbert

I dedicate this book to an inspirational, forgiving, and faithful God, my hardworking and encouraging
parents (Louis and Mary), loyal wife (Gretchen), five loving children (Aaron, Mikaela, Laura, Julia
and Gretchen, Jr.), and special brothers and sisters (Tom, Louis, Marylou, Ellen, Margaret and Peter).
You are all so very precious to me.

I also dedicate this book to all of the angels and kind friends (including the AEF board and staff)
who have believed in and helped me along the way to make my life wonderful and meaningful.

Al Louis Cecere

American Eagle Foundation
P.O. Box 333, Pigeon Forge, TN 37868
www.eagles.org • 1-800-2EAGLES

Text Copyright © 2005 American Eagle Foundation
Illustration Copyright © 2005 Gijsbert van Frankenhuyzen

Sleeping Bear Press
310 North Main Street, Suite 300
Chelsea, MI 48118
www.sleepingbearpress.com

THOMSON
★
GALE

© 2005 Thomson Gale, a part of the Thomson Corporation.

Thomson, Star Logo and Sleeping Bear Press are trademarks
and Gale is a registered trademark used herein under license.

Printed and bound in Canada.

10 9 8 7 6 5 4 3 2 1

Library of Congress Cataloging-in-Publication Data

Raven, Margot Theis.
Challenger : America's favorite eagle / written by Margot Theis Raven ;
illustrated by Gijsbert van Frankenhuyzen.
p. cm.
Summary: "Challenger is an American bald eagle raised by humans after failed
attempts to release him into the wild. He has become an ambassador who brings
attention to the plight of America's national bird"
—Provided by publisher.
ISBN 1-58536-261-1
1. Bald eagle—United States—Biography. I. Title.
QL696.F32R385 2005
598.9'43—dc22   2005017681

Illustrator's Acknowledgments

First and foremost, I wish to thank Al Cecere and everyone at the
American Eagle Foundation for sharing with me the wonders of
Challenger and all the other birds you work with at your amazing
facility. The Foundation has become an inspiring dream come true.
Thanks to Mrs. Brown and her summer Beehive class, to Nathan
Cooley (my nephew) and to all my friends and neighbors for
being my models. Special thanks go to John Rider, Eric Knorr,
Eugene King, Scott Wise, David Diamond, Kaz Kruszewski, and
V.J. Russell of the Air Force Band of Flight for becoming my
marching band in a pinch.

American Eagle Foundation's Acknowledgments

The AEF wishes to thank and acknowledge the following individuals
and organizations for their support: Dolly Parton, Bob Hatcher,
Carmen Simonton, James Rogers, Ken Bell, Judy Ward, Jack Hanna,
John Stokes, Ted Miller, Barbara Joines, The Dollywood Company
officers/staff, Tennessee Wildlife Resources Agency, U.S. Fish &
Wildlife Service and our generous member, volunteer, sponsor, donor,
entertainer, business, political, and sports supporters.

Special thanks to all the vigilant American heroes that worked so
hard to help bring back our magnificent national bird, the bald
eagle, from the brink of extinction.

We are grateful to Margot for creating a story with such colorful
and moving words, to Nick (Gijsbert) for painting beautiful and
inviting illustrations, and to Sleeping Bear Press staff for making
the book happen.

We hope you will all be pleased with and enjoy this children's story
about Challenger. He's already stirred the hearts and souls of many.
Thanks so much to all of you.

Foreword

I am often asked to write songs for recordings, television shows, and movies, but it is with great pleasure that I write the foreword to this book about the life of a very special eagle.

I have been known to kid around about the fact that Challenger is becoming a more popular celebrity than myself, but he really has become a very famous bird all across America. He will no doubt go down in history for his many important accomplishments.

The not-for-profit American Eagle Foundation (AEF), Challenger's caretakers, has been headquartered at the Dollywood entertainment park in Pigeon Forge, Tennessee, since 1991. They have done such great work to help restore and protect the U.S.A.'s living symbol of freedom, the bald eagle.

As part of their educational efforts, Challenger, Al Cecere, and the dedicated AEF staff have performed all over the nation at major sporting events, patriotic ceremonies, and school education programs, not to mention many guest appearances on national television.

This majestic bald eagle cannot survive in the wild on his own, but he has acted as a tremendous ambassador for his species in the wild and for our country. In doing so, he has lifted the spirits of many millions of people.

I am very proud of Challenger, Al, and the Foundation. I really hope that you enjoy their inspiring adventures within these pages.

Remember, we must all do our part to keep America's precious eagles flying strong and free for future generations.

Love, Dolly Parton

In a big stick nest atop a tall old pine, a bald eagle was born in a Louisiana woods. Snuggled deeply in the nest, the chick was too small to see the river below full of fish to eat. He did not know his mother and father returned to this same river and nest each year to lay new eggs and add more sticks until his home looked like a big woven basket in the clouds.

But for all the eaglet had yet to learn, he did know his sky world was full of song.

All day the chick heard the breeze in the pine and cypress trees, as it softly ruffled his new gray down. He heard his father's wings whir home after hunting for food. He heard his mother's beak shred fish into small bites to drop into his mouth. And he heard the music of wing-song. It was the flow of wind currents and warm thermals—an eagle's highway in the sky. Soon, that music would pull the eaglet to the rim of his nest to challenge the sky and fly!

But a great storm raged through the forest before
the chick could fly away from his home.

Wild winds pushed the nest to the ground with the frightened baby inside. The eaglet trembled on the forest floor as his parents hovered near to protect their baby from harm.

But when a fisherman came from the river, drawn by the sight of the giant nest on the ground, the eagles did not attack the man, for it is not an eagle's nature to fight humans.

As the eagles circled frantically, they watched the fisherman wrap their baby in his jacket and carry him home.

In the fisherman's house, the eaglet slept in a box softened with tissues. Many times a day, the family fed the chick as his eagle parents had, dropping bits of fish into the bird's open mouth.

The more the chick ate from human hands and saw the faces of his new feeders, the more he forgot his eagle parents. Soon, the chick even forgot he *was* an eagle! The little bird thought he was a person too—but nobody knew the chick had imprinted on humans.

When the fisherman's family could no longer care for the bird and knew he must return to the wild, they took him to a nearby zoo for further care.

In time, the eagle was taken to a hack tower—a nesting cage on tall tree-like poles—where he was fed by an unseen wildlife helper. At twelve weeks of age, the bird was fully grown. A human helper clipped a shiny identification band on the eagle's leg, then opened the cage door to release him to the wild. The young eagle leapt into the sky, gliding away on a breeze and thermals for the first time!

The wing-song was slow and easy that day, but when the bird (who still thought he was human) grew hungry, he did not know how to catch his own food. For many miles, the eagle flew on, searching for people to feed him.

"Look at that poor eagle!" folks at an Iowa Little League field gasped a week later. Starving, the young eagle landed near them, crying for a handout!

Reading the numbers on the bird's leg band, the people learned whom to call for help, and soon the eagle was back in the hack tower to regain his strength. Then once again he was released to the wild, but this time the hungry bird flew to a lake near Nashville, Tennessee, and was almost struck by a man who thought the bird had come to attack —not beg!

"Don't harm that eagle!" a kind person called out just in time.

Now, state and federal wildlife agencies sadly agreed, "This poor eagle can't survive on his own. He needs a home with humans—forever."

So it happened that the orphaned bird came to live in the foothills of the Great Smoky Mountains with a man named Al Cecere—a man who loved eagles.

Al began protecting the birds after seeing a newspaper photo of two dozen eagles shot by poachers. "Who would shoot an eagle?" he asked his wife, Gretchen. He was heartsick to learn bald eagles were endangered. They were nearly extinct, disappearing from America's skies due to human neglect and carelessness.

Al made a promise to keep eagles flying above. He wrote letters asking well-known people for help. He collected coins in containers outside of busy stores.

In time his cause grew and became the American Eagle Foundation. With support from Dollywood family park in Pigeon Forge, Tennessee, Al opened a large eagle sanctuary. There, Al rehabilitated, hatched, and released many birds of prey. He also gave injured (nonreleasable) ones a home, like the new eagle now in his care. Al and his staff called this bird "Challenger" in honor of the lost crew of the tragic space shuttle.

At first Al treated Challenger like other wild birds in his care. Then he saw this eagle didn't fly away when people came close. The eagle was curious and more social with humans than was normal. He turned his head from side to side, as if to see what a person might do next. Most unusual!

"You're not only a bird with nine lives and no broken wings, you're a miracle eagle—calm and comfortable around humans—but still true to your species." Al smiled at Challenger, realizing an exciting possibility. An eagle with perfect wings could be taught to fly freely before crowds, carrying the plight of all eagles to millions!

Al and his staff began training Challenger for that job. The eagle was friendly with humans when it came to food, but he was not a pet. Al gained Challenger's trust by having him hop to his gloved hand from a perch. Challenger got a small reward for the task—a tidbit of fish or quail.

Next, Challenger visited schools to educate children about protecting eagles and to get the bird used to noisy crowds. Sometimes a school bell might ring. Startled, Challenger would try to fly off, but Al used soft leather anklets and jesses on the bird's legs to keep him safely tethered to a glove or perch.

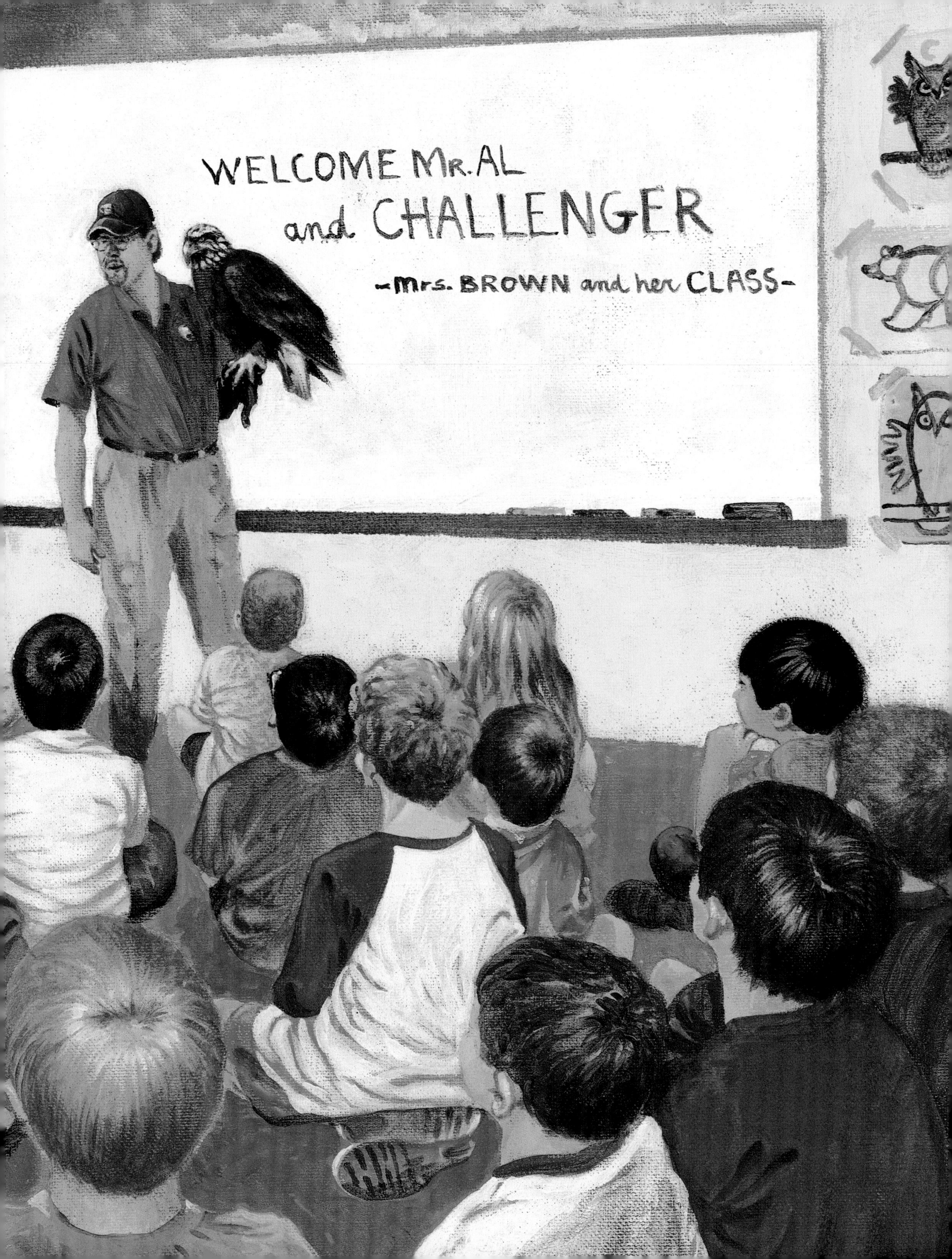
WELCOME Mr. AL
and CHALLENGER
-Mrs. BROWN and her CLASS-

Soon Challenger was flying
short distances at larger events, winging
about 100 feet on a long tethered line. More work
meant bigger food rewards. Challenger really liked that!

As Al and Challenger traveled far and wide, they learned to trust each other and became good friends. Challenger was a chatterbox from his baby begging days. In the van, Al would give a high whistle—"swheet swheet"— to speak to Challenger. The bird whistled and screeched back.

At night on the road, Al and Challenger watched television together in hotel rooms they shared.

Everywhere Al took Challenger, people loved the regal eagle. He learned to fly even longer distances, even in hotel ballrooms and a music theater, without being tethered. Free as a bird! One time, he even flew before 20,000 people in an enclosed arena. Al wondered: What else could this bird do?

Then Al heard of an event where Challenger could fly freely before 80,000 people in an outdoor stadium—to the national anthem! The event was the 1996 Para-Olympic Games for the world's best disabled athletes at Atlanta's Olympic Stadium. Flying there meant Challenger must soar from the torch—located *outside* the arena—over a parking lot—to land safely *inside* the stadium. It would be his longest flight since his time in the wild.

Anything could go wrong. Challenger could even get confused by all the noise and fly away!

Al's heart was torn. Nothing was more important than protecting Challenger; however, he believed the eagle could do it. Al went to Challenger's barn room to see if this special bird was truly ready to represent his fellow eagles.

Challenger sat proudly on his perch preening his soft brown breast feathers.

Then his noble white head turned sideways to look at Al, as if to say, *"I was born for this day!"*

Al knew that storm winds had blown the eagle from his nest, but he believed that winds of providence had brought Challenger to live with man—winds blowing through a country that had forgotten the eagle was a national symbol of trust between humans and all living creatures sharing the land. As eagles thrived in a healthy environment, so, too, would man survive on Earth.

The next day, Al called the producers of the Para-Olympic Games to suggest the flight. No trained eagle had ever flown freely before 80,000 people. It would be history in the making and shown on international television. But the producers were worried. Al asked for an audition and, like training an athlete, he conditioned Challenger's muscles to do the long flight. The bird performed so well that the producers said:
YES! Let's fly the eagle!

Challenger practiced with marching bands, waving flags, and jet planes flying overhead, preparing for the big event.

Challenger's people-crew practiced
their jobs, too. Pete stood at the base
of the flagpole to catch the bird on his
glove. Al swung the lure bag from a long
leather strap—with a whole quail attached—to draw
the eagle near and reward him for a good job. Jim stood high
up by the torch to release the bird when Al gave the signal.

During the opening ceremonies, a singer began
to sing "The Star-Spangled Banner."

Jim and Challenger looked
like specks high above by the torch.
Al had picked a note and word near the end of the song
to release the eagle, which timed forty-nine seconds of flight.

With a lump in his throat, Al signaled Jim by walkie-talkie: *Let Challenger fly!*

The eagle leapt from Jim's glove and took off, a blur of feathers over the cars parked below. Challenger didn't know that all eyes were on him, but he sensed a sound from long ago calling him to challenge the sky. It was the wing-song in the air!

"Look, an eagle!" people gasped, moved to tears when Challenger's wings swept into the stadium, lifting everyone in the spirit of the song's rising notes. "What a magnificent sight!" they cheered.

"Come on, Challenger, come on, boy!" Al and Pete called as Pete motioned with his gloved hand and Al swung the leather lure.

Then suddenly, Challenger had a plan of his own. He circled the flagpole three times...

...then talons forward and wings back, Challenger landed perfectly on Pete's glove—right on the anthem's last note!

How people roared! Al beamed with relief and pride but he couldn't speak. Challenger's soaring wings were words enough for a man who loved eagles.

On those wings, Al had just seen his dream to save all eagles take flight.

Epilogue

After the Para-Olympic Games flight, Al hung a big gold star on Challenger's barn door to say he was going to be one busy Eagle Ambassador from now on.

And he was! Challenger thrilled crowds at events from coast to coast. Announcers educated spectators before each flight about the important work this orphaned eagle was doing to save birds of prey.

However, not everything about the high-flying eagle was serious business. Some things were just fun. On one plane trip, the pilot told passengers he had "celebrity cargo" on board—A real bald eagle!

Challenger had fun experiences, too, appearing on television shows such as *Good Morning America* and *Jack Hanna's Animal Adventures*. He flew at NASCAR auto races, and at World Series baseball and Pro-Bowl football games. At Yankee Stadium he even sunned his feathers in the bull pen while watching pitchers warm up.

Challenger visited important places, too—the U.S. Capitol Building, the Pentagon, war memorials, and New York City's Ground Zero. His wings always inspired and healed spirits.

★ ★ ★